M000304879

VESPA:
AN ILLUSTRATED
HISTORY

VESPA: AN ILLUSTRATED HISTORY

Eric Brockway

Foulis

Haynes
®

© Eric Brockway 1993

All rights reserved. No part of this publication may be reproduced, stored in a retrieval system or transmitted, in any form or by any means, electronic, mechanical, photocopying, recording or otherwise, without prior permission in writing from G.T. Foulis & Co.

First published in 1993
Reprinted 1993, 1994 and 1995

A catalogue record for this book is available from the British Library.

ISBN 0 85429 892 4

Library of Congress catalog card no. 93-77251

G.T. Foulis & Company is an imprint Haynes Publishing, Sparkford, Nr. Yeovil, Somerset, BA22 7JJ, England

Typeset & Designed by G&M, Raunds, Northamptonshire, England
Printed in Great Britain by
Butler & Tanner Ltd, Frome and London

ACKNOWLEDGEMENTS

I would like to thank the many motorcycle and Vespa dealers throughout the United Kingdom and Commonwealth who gave me so much support during the three decades when I had the pleasure of heading a Douglas sales and service organization. None of the successes achieved would have been possible but for the assistance so generously given by the enthusiastic staff at the Kingswood works and latterly at Oak Lane, Fishponds, together with that of the officers and members of the Vespa Club of Great Britain and Veteran Vespa Clubs. I must not forget the many friends made within the Piaggio Company in Italy either. Unquestionably one of the highlights of my association with Douglas and Vespa was in 1974 when I was elected the first President of the newly formed Motor Cycle Association of Great Britain and the forerunner of the Motorcycle Industry Association.

It would be difficult to mention the names of all those dealers, trade organizations and trade colleagues with whom it has been my privilege to be associated over the years. I do feel, however, that I must make a special mention of some friends, as without their invaluable friendship my association with Vespa would not have been so pleasurable and memorable.

These names include Claude McCormack, André Baldet, E.O. (Blackie) Blacknell, William (Bill) Bond, Graeme Brown, Harold Briercliffe, George Baber, Charles Caswell, Ern. Hendy, Norrie Kerr, Ross McManus, Eddy Withers and all of my old Douglas area representatives.

I also wish to record all the help given by Jeff Clew and his enthusiasm for Douglas. Without his assistance and encouragement this book would not have been written.

Eric Brockway
Warmley
Bristol

INTRODUCTION
The Douglas Vespa Story

There surely can be no better time to reflect over the past 44 years than at the start of the fifth decade of the introduction into this country of the Vespa scooter, destined to become one of the most popular two-wheelers in the world.

My first sight of the Vespa (the Italian for 'wasp') was on the Douglas stand at the 1949 London Motor Cycle Show. Being one of the latest recruits to the famous Douglas motorcycle manufacturer's sales staff, I was somewhat sceptical as to its future here in what had always appeared to be a motorcycle country. I was soon to learn that whilst it was having its first public showing to the British public, it had been around in Italy some three years earlier. The real story began in Italy and concerned the distinguished Piaggio family of industrialists.

The Piaggio Company, established in 1884, began its activity in ship's furnishing, railways and aeronautical engineering fields. It took about 60 years before the Piaggio aircraft firm came up with all the right answers to design a two-wheeler, and then only as a result of some extremely accurate bombing by the Royal Air Force. They had half wrecked the huge Piaggio Aircraft Factory at Pontedera, leaving the staff with a number of headaches, not the least of these, paradoxically, being sore feet.

Getting from one part of the works to another was a tiring and time wasting business. To cut down the footwork, Dr Enrico Piaggio conceived the idea of a two-wheel vehicle and handed the problems over to his engineer, Corradino D'Ascanio. Born in Genoa on 22 February 1905, Enrico was the son of Senator Rinaldo Piaggio, founder of Piaggio in Genoa, who managed the Pontedera plant which made aircraft engines.

Scooters as we know them are not a post-war innovation, but were in fact the realization of a dream long ago. Ever since the turn of the century, motorcycle manufacturers had repeatedly tried to produce a machine which would combine at least part of the weather protection of a car with the handiness of the two-wheeler. Seen at the 1907 Stanley Show was the Max, and four years later at the Olympia Show the three-wheeler known as the Moto Frip, designed by Mrs Olive Kent. Many more followed. Again and again they failed, beaten by handling, cooling or structural problems. How then did Piaggio, with only the shell of a works, the usable parts of which were few and far between, get down to designing and producing what was to become the world's best-selling scooter?

Piaggio aircraft engineer D'Ascanio, trained and employed in the design of aircraft engines, had never worked on a two-wheeler before and had very little motorcycle experience. He tackled the problem from an engineering standpoint and within a few weeks his first design was ready.

Three of the main features that made the Piaggio design so distinctive and unique concerned the thought given by D'Ascanio to the overall engine concept. It was totally enclosed, unlike that of the motorcycle, the frame was open with a flat footboard, and the wheels were carried on stub axles. The combination of these three features was a stroke of genius on the part of the designer. He was, after all, first and foremost an aircraft designer with a lifetime's experience in air-cooled engines and stressed-skin framework construction.

D'Ascanio immediately settled for a two-stroke engine, not being concerned with high speeds. Through being familiar with chassisless structures he was far ahead of his day in considering them superior to conventional steel box or tube frames. The spot-welded frame used in all Vespas since 1946 is today common automobile practice and, to a lesser extent, that employed in racing motorcycles.

The engine was enclosed because again, ahead of his day, D'Ascanio realized that owners of such machines would look at them more as a means of transport than something to tinker with in their spare time.

He mounted the wheels on stub axles because he had seen motorcyclists mending punctures with all the attendant wheel removal problems. He decided that on his scooter the wheels would be mounted so that they could be removed without difficulty and, more importantly, without disturbing the drive to the rear wheel. Motorcycle designers, because they were practical men with little formal engineering training, had not been able

to bring their minds to this problem.

The most impressive of Engineer D'Ascanio's achievements was that he designed the Vespa from scratch, originating every component as he went along, yet he made the final assembly both a practicable machine-shop job and an economic sales proposition. Rarely has there been such a combination of vision and commercial acumen. By December 1945 his prototype had been tested and approved for production, and by April 1946 the Vespa was set for production.

And so the first Vespa scooter was born, an entirely new vehicle: so new that it might even strike the person who saw it for the first time as extremely ugly. Certainly the views expressed by conventional motorcyclists were far from complimentary. Fortunately Enrico Piaggio was not discouraged by the critics' remarks following the Vespa's first appearance on the Italian roads, for he quickly ordered its mass production.

The man responsible for bringing the Vespa to the UK was Claude McCormack, Managing Director of Douglas (Kingswood) Limited, famed for its motorcycles that have carried the name Douglas since 1907. At their Kingswood, Bristol, works, the company also manufactured industrial works trucks, engines, and electric road vehicles, and could boast a foundry that at one time was one of the largest in the area. To this day evidence of the castings that were produced in the Kingswood foundry can be seen with the maker's inscription on lamp posts, manhole covers and the like around the streets of east Bristol. When Claude McCormack took over as Managing Director of the Douglas plant in 1948 the company was in the hands of the Official Receiver. It was quite clear to McCormack that it could not possibly prosper unless some other type of production was introduced and the

Douglas motorcycle craftsmen kept employed.

So often in moments of crisis the solution comes out of the blue and so it was with the Douglas problem. Whilst relaxing in an Allasio cafe on an Italian holiday, with the work force back home very much in mind, McCormack saw a Vespa for the first time. With amazing foresight he felt that he had the solution to the problem. Call it a flash of inspiration or whatever you will, but it was followed by intense and immediate action on his part. Within a day or two he had plans in mind to build the Italian-designed Vespa at Kingswood.

When the imported models were displayed on Stand 64 at the 1949 Motor Cycle Show, it was by no means certain that the company would go ahead with the manufacture of the Vespa scooter under licence. There were still many obstacles to overcome, not the least of which was the fact that Douglas had a Receiver Manager appointed in October 1948, and there was a bank overdraft of some £657,000. On the same stand were also displayed the latest 350 cc Mark series and Plus model Douglas motorcycles, and there was some feeling amongst the trade, and to a lesser degree the public, as to whether Douglas had serious intentions to proceed with the production of a scooter. The model displayed was offered at a price of £128 0s 4d inclusive of purchase tax.

'Big Show Surprise — Britain to make Italian midget motorcycle' proclaimed the headlines in the *Daily Mail,* and the report in the *Bristol Evening World* of 1 November of a 'Big demand for Douglas scooters — £100,000 in orders' must have sounded like sweet music to the ears of the Douglas boss. The industrial correspondents really said it all in features that claimed Vespa and Ape (the three-wheeler version displayed) were names that were going to make history

in motorcycling. The first chapter might well have been concluded when Ronald Lombard, the General Sales Manager of the company, left the Motor Cycle Show with orders well over the £100,000 mark. The Vespa scooter certainly proved to be the show sensation of Earls Court that year.

The task of converting the orders into finished products was the next to be tackled, although the idea that Douglas would be in production at their Kingswood plant by the spring of 1950 was obviously too optimistic. There was much planning to be done apart from the resolution of the financial problem. However, the Receiver and Manager, Mr Walker, was obviously satisfied with the progress made since his appointment. Thanks to the reorganization that had been effected, coupled with an agreement with Piaggio to manufacture the Vespa under licence, the green light was given to proceed.

It really was a monumental task that was undertaken by the Douglas planners and technicians during the ensuing 16 to 17 months. Many exchanges of personnel proved necessary in connection with drawings as in those days staff were not so conversant with metric measurements. Numerous other difficulties were also encountered with tooling, plant and bought-in proprietary equipment. UK efforts were not helped by the terms of the licence which did not permit deviation from the Piaggio drawings. To avoid the high cost of expensive presses, certain pressings of the chassis and cowlings were imported direct from Piaggio.

In the automobile trade at the time there was a shortage of new cars, with petrol ration continuing. Claude McCormack, now a firm believer that his dream was about to come true, had just a little doubt about the amount of support that he was likely to receive from

These are to Certify that by direction of

His Royal Highness
The Prince Philip, Duke of Edinburgh

I have appointed

Douglas (Kingswood) Ltd.,

into the place and quality of

Suppliers of Vespa Scooters

to His Royal Highness

To hold the said place until this Royal Warrant shall be withdrawn or otherwise revoked.

This Warrant is granted to

Eric F. Brockway, Esq.,

trading under the title stated above and empowers the holder to display His Royal Highness Arms in connection with the Business but does not carry the right to make use of the Arms as a flag or trade mark.

The Warrant is strictly personal to the Holder and will become void and must be returned to the Treasurer to His Royal Highness in any of the circumstances specified when it is granted.

Given under my hand and Seal this Tenth day of June 1967.

Treasurer to The Duke of Edinburgh.

In 1967 Douglas were awarded a Royal Warrant for the supply of Vespa scooters to HRH Prince Philip.

motorcycle dealers, so he sought after and successfully obtained the support of a number of reputable car dealers who were prepared to 'have a go'. It had not been difficult to dispose of the first batch of imported machines, and whilst there appeared to be a certain amount of scepticism and reluctance on the part of some motorcycle dealers it was not long before they became aware of the interest being shown by car dealers who had so readily accepted the Vespa.

Imported models of the 125 cc Vespa were soon to be seen in the London showrooms of Rolls Royce dealer H.A. Fox & Co. Ltd, Rootes dealers University Motors, and in the provinces by car dealers who never before had sold two-wheelers. Support was also given by two-wheel stalwarts such as Blacknell Motors of Nottingham, Hallens of Cambridge, Kings Motors of Oxford, Withers of West Norwood, London, the J.R. Alexander Group of Scotland, G.D. Brown of Godalming, T. Cowie of Sunderland and the Cope and Colmore Groups from the Midlands. All had sufficient faith in the company and the new product to take it on, and on reflection must surely have been delighted with the decision to do so. It must, of course, be said that these remarks apply to the period when only imported models were available and not when production got under way at Kingswood. By then the support from all dealers was quite remarkable.

It is sad to record here that the success of the Vespa scooter did not apply to the Ape commercial three-wheeler which had been displayed alongside it at Earls Court. A mere handful of this type of vehicle with various commercial bodies fitted were imported by Douglas but production of it was never undertaken in the UK. Piaggio appointed other concessionnaires to handle it there.

With no Motor Cycle Show in 1950 and the pressure of a determined Receiver and Manager to ensure better financial results were forthcoming, the launch on 15 March 1951 of the first Douglas-produced Vespa was truly a memorable event. In itself it proved a great experience for those who recognized just what success or failure meant. The ceremony took place at the Kingswood works when the Lord Major of Bristol, Alderman F.A. Parish, received the first 125 cc 'Rod' model Vespa from the Douglas production line and handed it to Miss Charmaine Innes, a well-known star of stage, radio and television at that time.

The Douglas-made 'Rod' model, as it was later to become affectionately known (on account of its rod-operated controls), was now ready to set a new fashion in the two-wheeler world. The events and happenings associated with the Vespa scooter over the years will by now have become legendary by virtue of the many millions who have experienced scooter riding.

History will certainly record that the introduction of the Vespa scooter to the roads of this country and its appearance in the dealers' showrooms exploited a new market. The success that followed was unforeseen, overwhelming and almost uncontrollable. The first to be won over by the new mode of transport were, in the main, the professional classes — no young person in 'better off' society would consider him or herself complete without a Vespa. A motor car was out of the reach of most young people, so the Vespa scooter took its place.

The milestones along the 44 years that followed that proud day in November 1949, when Claude McCormack saw the fruition of his holiday dream, need few additional words. The camera has recorded most of them, as the following reflections will reveal.

The Douglas stand at the 1949 Earls Court Motor Cycle Show. On display for the first time in the UK was the imported Piaggio-made Douglas Vespa. The three-wheeled Ape with the enclosed van type body is seen on the left. The 1950 range of Douglas 350 cc motorcycles was also displayed.

An aerial view of the impressive Piaggio Pontedera plant taken in the early 1970s. In the background can be seen the old runway.

Left Dott. Enrico Piaggio, the man responsible for the creation of the Vespa scooter.

Born in Genoa on 22 February 1905, the son of Senator Rinaldo Piaggio, founder of Piaggio & Co, he studied in Genoa and obtained a degree in Economics and Commerce with later specialization in German Universities. He joined the family business in 1928 as Manager of the Pontedera plant which produced aircraft engines. Under his management the plant began to develop and in six years the work force grew from 136 to 6,950.

Dott. Piaggio succeeded his father as Managing Director upon the latter's death in 1938. The following year, the first four-engined P 108 bombers were built. During the Second World War more than 10,000 workers were engaged on war work at the Pontedera plant.

In 1951, the University of Pisa conferred upon Dott. Piaggio the Honorary Degree of Engineering. He died in 1965. Many present on 28 April 1956 to celebrate the production of the millionth Vespa at Pontedera were smilingly invited to join him again for the production of the five millionth Vespa, an appointment that sadly could not be fulfilled.

Above right The original Piaggio-manufactured Vespa scooter was produced at the Pontedera works in 1946. It is interesting to compare this model with the 125 cc Vespa in the following photograph that appeared on the Douglas stand at the 1949 London Motor Cycle Show.

Right The first prototype Douglas-built Vespa had the headlamp fitted on the front mudguard. When the production of Douglas-manufactured models commenced in 1951 the position of the headlamp was raised to that of a mounting on the front apron, as shown in the following photograph.

Above *A head-on view of the production Douglas Vespa showing the revised headlamp mounting on the apron and the Douglas Vespa badge.*

Below *A number of trips to the Piaggio Pontedera plant were arranged for Douglas dealers to see the production of Vespa scooters and the following series of photographs show UK dealers on such a visit in 1966. This is the press shop.*

Above right *A closer shot of one of the giant presses that transformed sheets of steel into part of the chassis.*

Below right *Chassis assembly.*

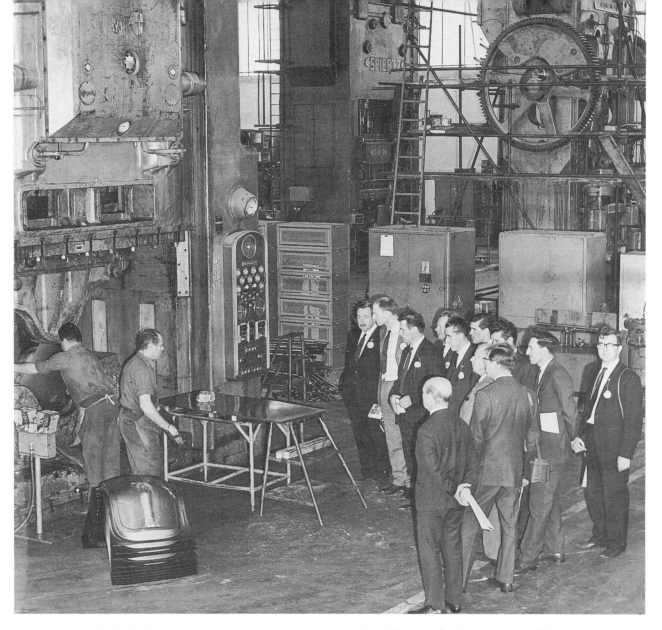

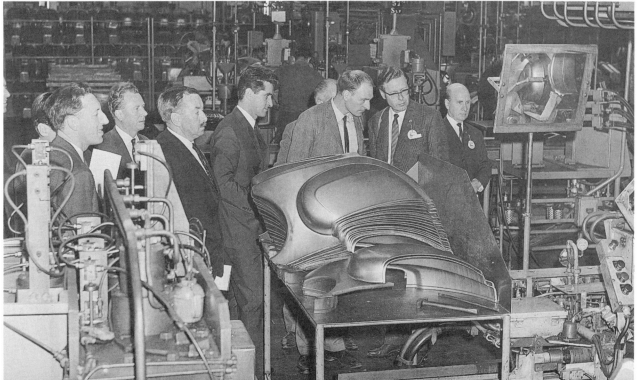

Left *Always an interesting part of the Vespa production is a machine being put through the roller test. Here is a 90SS being tested to simulate the effects of it being driven on the road with gear changing, etc.*

Below left *A view of the Vespa final assembly line showing the overhead conveyor.*

Right *Claude McCormack, whose foresight led to the Vespa being introduced and manufactured by Douglas in the United Kingdom.*

Below *An aerial view of the Douglas works in Kingswood, showing the extensive sports ground on the right, now a company car park and containing an extension to the works buildings. The Hanham Road office block can be clearly seen in the foreground, behind which is the foundry.*

Amongst the invited guests to the launch of the Douglas Vespa in March 1951 was actress Charmaine Innes, seen here astride a 'Rod' model after receiving it from the Mayor of Bristol.

The first Vespa destined for the export market. The Mayor of Bristol, Alderman A.F. Parish, shares in a joke with the photographer although he quickly removed his top hat when the packers moved in. Considerable numbers of machines were exported to Australia and New Zealand.

An unusual view of a batch of machines packed for rail transport.

This rider's view of the handlebar layout shows the rod and universal joint system of gear changing through the swivelling left-hand control lever. The right-hand twist grip was the throttle control, to the left of which was a thumb switch controlling the lights and horn and containing the engine cut-out button.

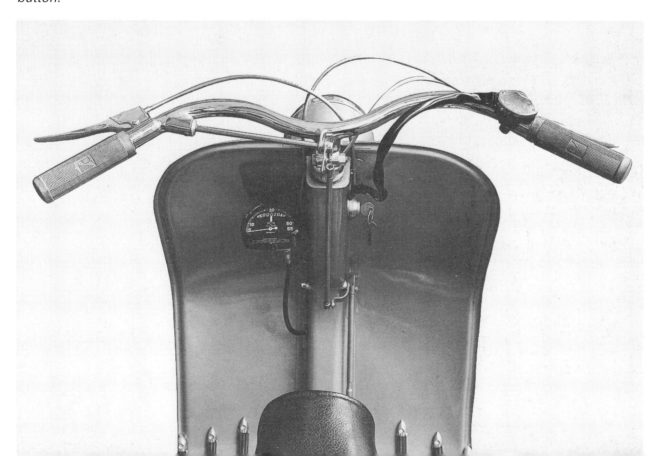

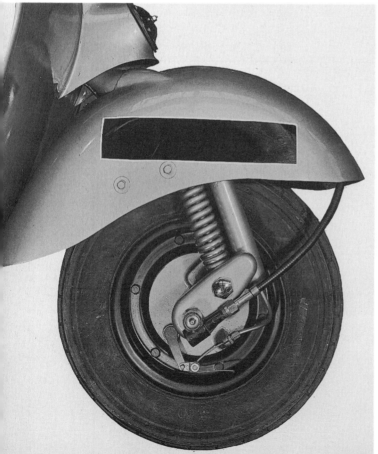

Above *Access to the 'Rod' model engine was easily gained by depressing a spring catch on the engine wing or cowling and allowing the attachment link to be raised.*

Left *3.50 x 8 in tyres were fitted to the 125 cc 'Rod' model, quickly detachable and interchangeable following normal car practice. Tyre changes were effected with simplicity by separating the two wheel flanges. This shot of the front wheel shows the suspension unit.*

Above right *The foundry at the Douglas, Kingswood works, was at one time one of the largest in the area and shown here is a section where the light alloy castings for the Vespa engine bearer and cylinder heads were gravity die cast. It was here in Kingswood that the Douglas Brothers commenced their foundry business in 1882.*

Right *In the semi-automatic machine shop a number of BSA machines were used. Here can be seen Vespa crankshafts, gear clusters, cylinder barrels and brake drums ready for machining.*

Infra-red paint drying equipment in use at the Kingswood plant. The machine components entering the drying room tunnel are the chassis, lamp shells, steering columns with front mudguard, engine cowlings and fan covers.

All engines were tested prior to final assembly and road testing. Certain engines were never assembled into finished machines after being bench tested for a specific number of hours. The components from those engines, after dismantling, were passed to the laboratory and inspection departments for further testing.

The final assembly line. Maybe not quite such an impressive line as its Piaggio counterpart but adequate to meet the demand for home sales requirements.

Considerable support was given by the company to their nationwide dealer network in order to provide the specialized service sought by Vespa owners. Student mechanics from throughout the UK were instructed in the use of special service tools as can be seen in this picture of the Dealer Vespa Training School at the works. A range of the special service tools can be seen on the bench in the foreground.

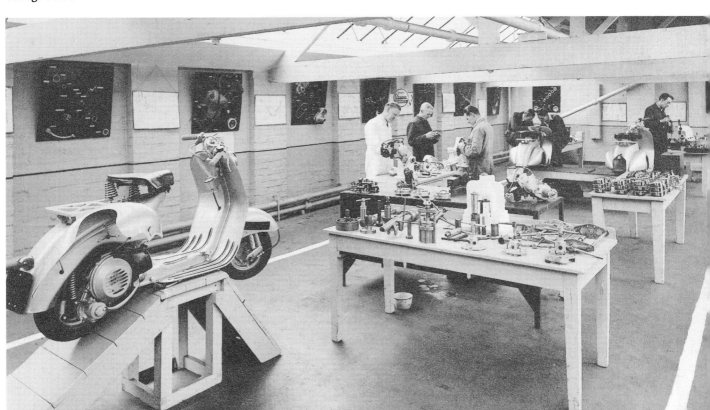

Some London Pearly Kings and Queens seen trying a new mode of transport, of which they appear to approve.

Actress Phylis Adriene astride a Vespa, with Bill Powell and a 1921 Douglas motorcycle in front of the grandstand on the company sports ground in 1951.

It was soon to be discovered that the new mode of transport presented a golden opportunity to publicize both rider and machine. In the following selection of photographs can be seen how many well-known personalities in all walks of life were photographed with a Vespa.

Above *Many screen actors and actresses enjoyed riding scooters both in private and during film making. Here are seen film star Gregory Peck posing for a publicity 'still', with Audrey Hepburn and pillionist Eddie Albert waiting for the 'dicky bird'.*

Right *Henry Fonda with a Vespa GS model which was never produced by Douglas, even though it proved to be one of the most popular imported machines.*

Left *A picture to make almost every teenage girl — and many not-so-teenage girls — squeal with envy. There on the pillion of lucky Lorna Deane's brand new Sportique model is pop star Cliff Richard. Lorna won the scooter and met Cliff in Blackpool as part of her prize in a nationwide ABC competition in connection with the film Summer Holiday in 1963.*

Below *No caption is really necessary as the picture tells it all. The Vespa 90 was part of her prize for winning the Miss Darling competition.*

Right *Here Anne Turner, who won the 1966 Miss Vespa Darling competition and a 90 model scooter, is seen receiving the Silver Rose bowl from actor Roger Moore (The Saint). Miss Vespa Competitions at Vespa Club events were highly successful. Winners of regional rallies met in the final held at the Annual Super National Rally.*

Below right *Motor racing champion Stirling Moss enjoyed his outings on a Vespa scooter. Here he is seen taking delivery of a 150 New Line model.*

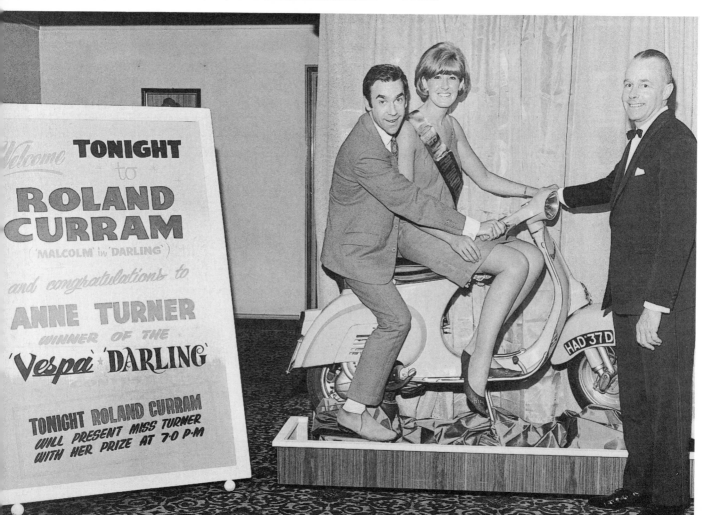

Left *In October 1960 a 125 model was donated to the Appeal of the London Association for the Blind Fund and show business people played in a football match on the Brentford City ground. Over £700 was raised and the following photographs show some of the Jack Hawkins and Friends XI as well as the Show Business and TV All-Star Personalities XI. Here Jack Hawkins, star of television, screen and stage tries out the Vespa for himself.*

Above *John Gregson, a member of the Show Business team.*

Left *Here are seen two very well known personalities: Eric Sykes with comedian Jack Jackson in the role of pillion passenger.*

Left *Star of one of the successful 1960 television series,* For the Love of Mike, *Michael Medwin, a member of the Show Business XI.*

Below *Stars in the 1963 Bristol Hippodrome pantomime were Morecambe and Wise, seen here in relaxed mood on a visit to the Douglas works. They appear to be having fun astride two 'Rod' models being prepared for the 1964 Veteran Vespa Rally.*

Right *A highly successful tie-up with a French film* The Heat of the Summer *introduced a new French star, Patricia Karim, and provided a good opportunity to publicize the French-made 125 ACMA Vespa seen here with the new star. At the London launch of the film on 6 November 1959 some 600 members of the Vespa Club were seen to be parked outside the Tottenham Court Road Cinema.*

Left *The winner of this Vespa in a competition sponsored by the* Bournemouth Evening Echo *to promote the film* No, My Darling Daughter *was delighted to be invited to ride pillion to Ken Dodd, the well-known comedian who made the presentation. A Vespa featured prominently throughout the film.*

Below *Comedian Alfred Marks plays to the gallery on a 42L2 model displayed on the 1956 Motor Cycle Show stand.*

Right *An elegant pose by two stars — West End stage and film actress Elizabeth Larner, star of* Kismet *at the Stoll Theatre, with a 42L2 Vespa — star of the 1956 Show. She is chatting with the Vespa Club general secretary, William Bond, who provides the supporting role.*

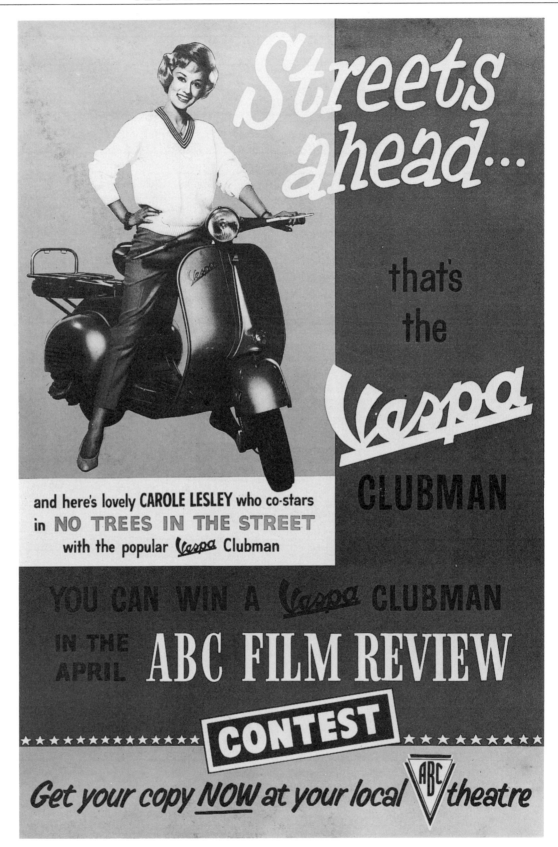

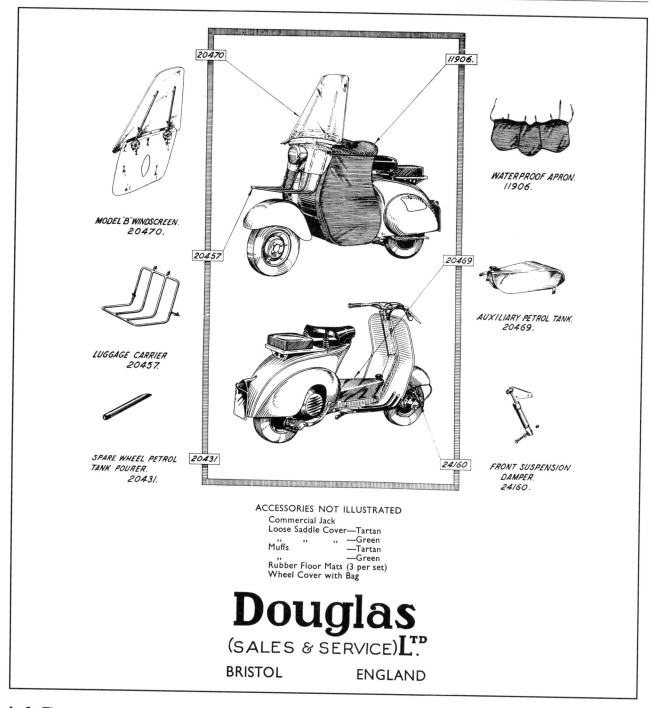

MODEL "B" WINDSCREEN.
20470.

LUGGAGE CARRIER
20457.

SPARE WHEEL PETROL
TANK POURER.
20431.

WATERPROOF APRON.
11906.

AUXILIARY PETROL TANK.
20469.

FRONT SUSPENSION
DAMPER.
24160.

ACCESSORIES NOT ILLUSTRATED
Commercial Jack
Loose Saddle Cover—Tartan
      ”   ”   ”   —Green
Muffs   ”   —Tartan
      ”   —Green
Rubber Floor Mats (3 per set)
Wheel Cover with Bag

Douglas
(SALES & SERVICE) LTD
BRISTOL   ENGLAND

Left *The company spent considerable sums of money annually on publicity and there were many successful promotions in which a machine was used. A good example is the tie up with the promotion of an ABC Film Review contest in which a Clubman model was used as the prize in the April 1959 competition. Here is a copy of the poster for the film* No Trees in the Street *which starred actress Carole Lesley.*

Above *The company offered a wide range of accessories designed specifically for the Vespa, most being of a functional nature. Here is a page from a Douglas accessory leaflet issued for the earlier models.*

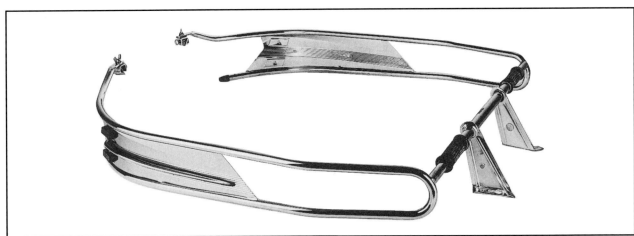

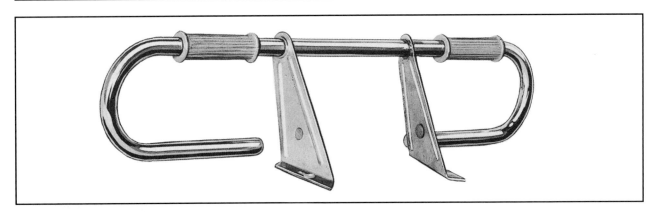

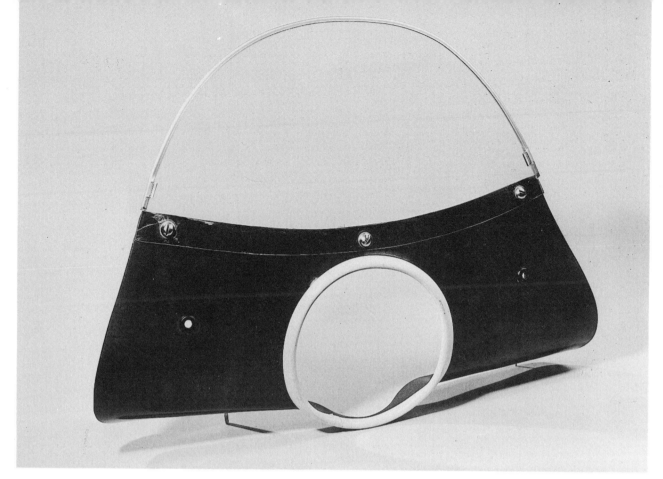

Top left *Here are illustrated a number of accessories fitted to a machine and on the following pages a selection of accessories designed for specific models.*

Middle left *One of the more popular accessories for the owners of the 152L2, Sportique, 160GS, GL and SS models was the all round New Yorker footrest and crashbar.*

Bottom left *The footrest and combined crashbar suitable for the 152L2, 150 Standard, Sportique and 160GS models.*

Above *There were many different types of windscreens and whilst owners of the earlier models preferred the large screen, the flyscreen type illustrated here was for use with the Sportique and 160GS machines, the coloured fairing proving very popular.*

Right *A popular accessory for the 152L2, 150 Standard, Sportique, 160GS and 150GL machines was this horn cover and steering column embellishment.*

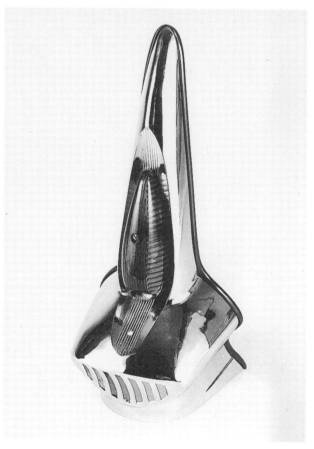

The company became renowned for its Motor Cycle Show stands over the years. One of the more impressive was that of the Vespa seemingly supported by a stream of water gushing from an ornamental arrangement in a garden pool at the 1952 Show.

On the 1954 stand visitors were puzzled at the sight of a 'dumb blonde' astride a Vespa doing a tightrope act. No hands, wires or stays, there the Vespa and young lady swayed to and fro whilst members of the public stood and tried to fathom out just how it was done.

Unable to open the 1956 Show as planned, Her Royal Highness the Duchess of Gloucester paid a lightning visit later in the week. Seen here, she was somewhat intrigued by the 'magic' Vespa on a wire entering and leaving a garage.

At the 1958 Show visitors saw a slight change of mood when the Latin Quarter lovelies attired in Edwardian costumes visited the Douglas stand. The modern miss preferred a Vespa whilst not unexpectedly the Edwardian miss chose a 1907 Douglas V4 motorcycle.

Left *The star attraction on the 1960 stand was a 152L2 model Vespa mounted on a revolving glass jewel.*

Below left *Probably one of the most impressive displays, if not the largest, was the giant Vespa New Line model standing 12 ft high, the centrepiece of the 1979 Douglas Motor Cycle Show stand. The author, flanked by members of his sales and service team, poses in front of the Vespa — one for the family album. Seated on the dualseat can be seen C.E. (Titch) Allen, B.E.M., Founder of the Vintage Motor Cycle Club.*

Right *A little glamour with the aid of one of the company models used to publicize their products, with the added attraction of a personal appearance of famous World Motorcycle Racing Champion, Mike Hailwood. They make a striking picture beside the giant machine at the 1979 Motor Cycle Show.*

In 1981, the International Motor Cycle Show was staged for the first time at the National Exhibition Centre, Birmingham, and the centrepiece of the Douglas/Piaggio stand was once again the giant Vespa model. On the stand were also displayed the Bianchi range of bicycles as well as a new range of mopeds, products of Piaggio and associated companies, which were also marketed by Douglas.

With the interest being shown by tradesmen, the introduction of the 125 cc G models (indicating a cable gear change) suggested that the company should turn its attention to providing not only a commercial sidecar outfit but also the supply of sidecar gears for solo machine conversion. Illustrated is the standard Vespa Commercial. For the technically minded reader the capacity of the box sidecar was 6.75 cu ft, which permitted a 125 lb payload. It was built in aluminium sheeting with the lid hinged at the front and provided with a lock at the rear. The commercial box and fitting cost £35 with no purchase tax.

Another illustration of the versatility of the Vespa commercial displayed by a dealer. We hope he proved his point!

The sidecar attached to this 125 cc Vespa illustrates a rather novel manner of advertising a well-known brand of bread, at the same time putting it to good use as a delivery vehicle. The machine performed well with a cruising speed of 35 mph and a petrol consumption of between 65 and 70 mpg was claimed.

Left *Established British sidecar manufacturers, Watsonian and Blacknell, soon showed an interest in providing tailor-made passenger sidecars. Pictured here is a Watsonian-made outfit fitted to a 150GS, dual toned to match the machine.*

Below *Here is shown a passenger sidecar from the German manufacturer Steib. The owner of this combination was obviously a member of the 'ride in all weathers' brigade, with a continental-style windscreen and apron fitted to his machine.*

Right *The company did not have success with the light motor-truck style three-wheeler Ape, designed for small and rapid deliveries, especially in city centres. Traders preferred the already well-established Minivan four-wheelers. Apart from importing a small number, four examples of which are shown in a page from the sales leaflet, the company withdrew from this market to concentrate on solos and mopeds. Piaggio made a new appointment for the three-wheeler franchise.*

TECHNICAL SPECIFICATIONS

Engine: 2 stroke 7.63 cu. in. displacement - maximum power 4 HP at 4500 r. p. m.

Transmission gear ratios: 4 speed.

Starting: By hand-lever operated by driver while seated.

Engine cooling: By forced air blown by a centrifugal fan.

Frame: of pressed steel sheet electrically welded.

Transmission: with differential and chain drive

Suspension: coiled steel springs on front wheel. Elastic torsion bars and hydraulic shock-absorbers for rear wheels.

Wheels: wheels are easily dismantled in a manner similar to automobile wheels. All wheels are interchangeable.

Tires: PIRELLI low pressure 4.00 × 8.
pressure for front wheel: 15 lb/sq. in.
pressure for rear wheels: 21 lb/sq. in.

Brakes: hydraulic brakes on rear wheels, operated by pedal. Mechanically operated brake on front wheel. Parking brake on the transmission; operated by hand lever.

Lights: three front lights: one bright headlight of the two beam intensity type; and two dim lights on the sides. One red tail of standard type. Electric power is supplied by the generator integral with the flywheel type magneto, connected to a battery.

Truck body: of wood with supporting ribs, the rear board is hinged.

Overall length	95.7 in.
width	50.9/16 in.
Maximum height	37.13/16 in.
Height of seat above ground	27 in.
Height of running board above ground	5.15/16 in.
Minimum turning circle diameter	74.2/8 in.
Wheel base	40.1/2 in.
Height of platform above ground	19.7 in.
Truck body dimensions	43.11/16 × 43.11/16 in.
Height of side panels	8.11/16 in.
Empty weight	300 lbs.
Useful load	450 lbs.
Maximum speed on level run	25 m.p.h.

Hill-climbing ability: 18 % up grade with full load.

Consumption: 80 miles per gallon, according to the amount of load carried.

Above *It is not possible within the limitations of this book to cover in any great detail all the models that were imported or manufactured by the company, although it is important to record some of the features of a number of the models that upheld the popularity of the Vespa over the past 44 years. The G models, introduced in October 1953, incorporated several new features, the more apparent of which related to the gear change mechanism. Replacing the rod by a cable enclosed in a neat rubber casing resulted in a more flexible and positive gear change. The speedometer mounting was also changed and there was a new footbrake, petrol filler cap, rear lamp and number plate.*

The GL2 shown here followed, and in a Motor Cycle *road test of 9 December 1954 the tester compared the machine with one tested in January 1952. His report contained the following comments: 'The engine of the latest model has been extensively redesigned to provide longer life and improved cooling. Another important modification concerns the clutch, which has been rendered virtually indestructible by the adoption of two additional plates. For the first time, a smartly styled dualseat is available at extra cost.'*

Left *In the same 1954* Motor Cycle *road test, the GL2 was also described as a 'lively runabout with good weather protection; easy to ride and clean'. Here is illustrated a GL2 model and just what the best dressed scooter rider was wearing in 1955.*

Thought by many scooter riders to be one of the most exciting Vespas to be imported by the company — the 150GS. The Series 1 was introduced in 1955 to meet the demand for a bigger, faster Vespa. This model had a four-speed gearbox, bigger bore and stroke engine, increased tank capacity, 10 inch wheels, a new handlebar layout and a new dualseat. Finished in silver it made a welcome addition to the range of Douglas-produced 125 cc models.

The introduction of the 42L2 and 92L2 models saw many changes in the mid-1950s, amongst them a new crankshaft, flywheel magneto, clutch and silencer. There was also a new headlamp layout, speedometer, light switch and suspension unit.

There now appeared to be a demand for a 150 cc standard model to be introduced into the Vespa range and to fill this gap a very limited number of the Continental model (shown here) were imported, to be followed in March 1957 by the Standard 150 cc model. The new model had a 'square' type engine (57 mm bore x 57 mm stroke), bridged transfer ports, a deflector-type piston and a new carburettor. At the same time as the 150 model was introduced, the company also announced that production of the 125 model was being stepped up.

To meet the demand from many members of the now well-established Vespa Club, the company continued to import the GS models. The VS2, 3 (the German version) 4 and 5 Series and the VD2TS followed. The advantage of importing these models was that whereas production at the Kingswood plant was confined to one capacity machine, with limited output, Piaggio were able with their much greater production capacity and implementation of modifications to supply the UK with machines that were up to date in both design and performance.

Vintage Motor Scooter Club enthusiast Bill Drake is the proud owner of this Series VS4, considered by many to be the thoroughbred Vespa when imported in 1958. Note the fixing of the spare wheel and the quickly detachable spare petroil container, just in case the fuel tank reserve was insufficient to make it to the next filling station! Bill Drake is the current treasurer of the Vintage Motor Scooter Club, an International Club for Vintage Scooter enthusiasts. The Chairman is Ian Harrop, also Editor of the club magazine. All makes of scooters are catered for and there are members delegated to provide specialist information. Bill looks after Vespa riders in the Club.

Probably one of the most important highlights in the history of the company since the 'Rod' model first rolled off the Kingswood production line was the introduction of the 150 cc Clubman model. It was introduced by Claude McCormack at the October 1957 Dealer Convention. Here the stage is all set at the Grand Hotel, Bristol, where some 350 dealers saw the new Clubman model for the first time.

It was now becoming apparent that a number of Douglas dealers were anxious to become much more involved in the promotion of the machine in which they had so much faith so it is worth recording a few of their exploits.

Amongst the now legendary names of Vespa scooterists surely that of Frenchman André G.J. Baldet must be at the top of the list. I first met this dynamic person in Northampton, his adopted home, in the early days of the production of the Vespa at Kingswood. Whilst it can be said that André is typically French, there has always been something about his determination to succeed with his many ventures here that typifies the British spirit. All those who know André well will understand why any job that demands exercising his very own indeterminable enthusiasm for leadership and professionalism is undertaken so well.

It was in 1955 that his dream of opening his own business came to reality. Moto Baldet opened in Northampton and a year later he was appointed a Douglas main dealer. The Moto Vespa showroom in Northampton was amongst the first exclusively Vespa showrooms in the UK. One of my proudest possessions to this day is a green £1 note signed by André in 1955. I won it from him as the result of a bet made that I would be sitting in his office by 9 am to discuss the question of a Vespa agency with him! I was there on time and won!

Above *André Baldet's love of stunts using a Vespa is well-known. Together with scooter accessory specialist Ken Cobbing, in 1957 he completed a 720 mile coast-to-coast run in 24 hours. Here Baldet is seen being greeted by Charles Cruickshank, the Bristol dealer.*

Left *In 1958 André successfully completed a 3,620 mile tour of Europe covering nine countries in ten days on a Clubman and sidecar. Throughout the whole trip he was accompanied by a Shell-Mex film unit and was the star of the film Tough on a Two-stroke.*
Here the author is seen congratulating André on the completion of his trip which took in five Vespa factories on the Continent. On the last day of the trip adverse weather conditions were comparable with those of the Monte Carlo Rally and snow can be seen in this photograph, taken in London.

Above *André Baldet's claim, 'We ride 'em as well as sell 'em' certainly proved a point when he won the 1958 I.O.M. Scooter Rally Concours d'Elegance with his GS. He is seen here in the line up with other Vespa competitors.*

Right *Later in 1958, André and Manxman Dennis Christian set out to lap the famous Isle of Man TT course continuously for four days and four nights to carry out one of the most rigorous tests ever made at that time on a scooter. 100 laps of the 37.75 mile mountain circuit in 100 hours were achieved, with a quarter of an hour in hand. The total distance travelled on the 150 Arc en Ciel GS was 3,775 miles in 99 hours 41 minutes 8 seconds. André and Dennis kept up continuous four-hour shifts during the test and for the final victory lap Dennis rode on the pillion. The riders were presented with a certificate of Meritorious Performance by the Isle of Man Scooter Association.*

THE ISLE OF MAN MOTOR SCOOTER ASSOCIATION
CERTIFICATE OF MERITORIOUS PERFORMANCE

THIS IS TO CERTIFY that 100 consecutive laps of the famous T.T. Mountain Circuit in the Isle of Man were completed by a 150c.c. 1958 Arc en Ciel G.S. Vespa Motor Scooter ridden by Mr Andre Baldet and Mr Dennis Christian on behalf of Messrs. Moto Baldet of Northampton. This is the first time that such a unique feat has been performed on a motor scooter. The test commenced on Monday, 18th August, 1958 at 14·00 hours and finished on Friday, 22nd August, 1958 at 17·41·08 hours, during which period the Vespa machine concerned covered 100 laps of the course, a total distance of 3,775 miles in 99 hours, 41 minutes 8 seconds.

Weather conditions could not have been worse. Rain fell almost continuously during the test and fog on the mountain sections of the course reduced visibility to 5 yards, which made arduous demands on both riders and observers.

Replenishment – Was carried out at the T.T. Grandstand. Shell petrol and oil was used throughout the test – also Lodge plugs and Pirelli tyres.

Adjustments – during the test the following adjustments were made:– New headlamp glass fitted. Replacement of inner clutch cable.

At the conclusion of the test the machine was officially examined by Mr. Eagles, A.C.U. Official Measurer and found to conform in every way to the manufacturers catalogued specification.

Jeff Bain Chairman, Isle of Man Motor Scooter Association.

E.Battye Secretary

W.F. Farrow Official Timekeeper.

Karl Eagles A.C.U. Official Measurer

Left *A weekend in Paris for £10 was the next stunt undertaken by André Baldet. Leaving London after a day's work one Friday in April 1961, Jean Harris, along with Jon Stevens, the Editor of* Scooter World, *joined André on the night boat to Dunkirk, scootered through France to Paris, did some sightseeing with the Vespa Club of Paris members, and was back in London on the Sunday to be ready for work on the Monday. Total cost for each was under £10. They ate well, stayed in a hotel and did the return Channel crossing by air from Le Touquet.*

Right *Another dealer with the flare for showing the world just what could be achieved with a scooter was Welling dealer Artie Shaw. On April Fool's Day 1959, along with one of his assistants, Artie succeeded in beating the Golden Arrow express to Paris. Leaving Victoria Station at 1 pm, the same time as the train, he arrived in Paris at 7.50 GMT astride a Vespa GS, some 50 minutes ahead of a fellow Vespa dealer from Folkestone who had made the journey by train. Seen here is Artie, ready to leave Victoria Station astride his GS. The gentleman appearing to be so unconcerned about the whole affair is none other than Chelsea pensioner, C.S.M. Shaw — Artie's father.*

Below *André, Jon Stevens and Jean Harris, the teenage daughter of Bovey Tracey, Devon, dealer Ken Harris, show a French rail official their plans for the £10 trip to Paris beside the London-Paris night express. The machines used were a 1959 125 which André had prepared in his* Arc en Ciel *colours, whilst Jean and Jon were on 125 Standard models.*

Left *Artie Shaw (**right**) wishes Jack Canini, the Folkestone Vespa dealer, bon voyage before their separate departures to Paris.*

Right *Another event inspired by Kent dealer, Artie Shaw, to coincide with the launch of the 150GL, was an 850 mile Four Capital Cities Safety Run. It helped counter to some extent the rather depressing figures released by the Ministry of Transport in 1964 showing that more deaths and injuries were caused by road accidents than in any other peace year, and supported the National Two-Wheeler week held in 1965. Four riders astride two 150GL models took part, calling on and collecting messages from the Chief Constable of Bristol, the Road Safety officers of Cardiff, City of Westminster, London, Glasgow and the Accident Prevention Officer, Edinburgh. They were delivered to the Road Safety Officer at Blackpool on the opening day of Blackpool Motor Cycle Show. From left to right in the picture are Artie Shaw and sales assistant Robert Lee, Roy Gibbons and Mike Murphy, members of the Vespa Club of Britain, being welcomed on their arrival at the Blackpool show.*

Below *One of the best known Douglas dealers in the London area for both motorcycles and Vespas was Withers of 88 Knights Hill, West Norwood. This early photograph of the premises shows two 'Rod' models on the forecourt with the different types of windscreen that will be familiar to many thousands of Vespa owners.*

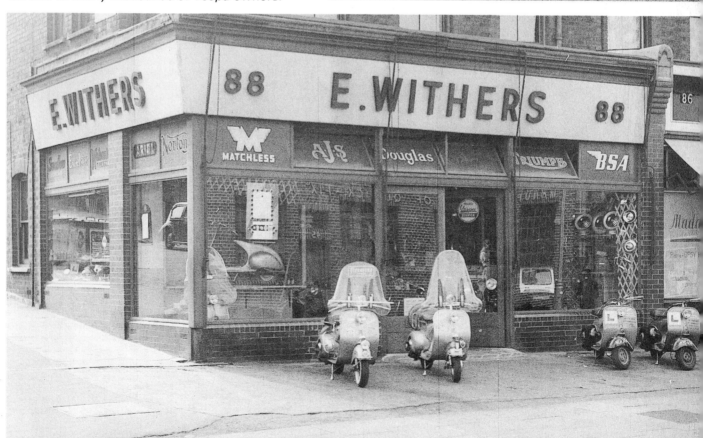

Above *Other versions of the Sportique model followed towards the end of 1962 when sales began to fall, and a variant known as the Sportique Supreme was introduced. Finished in polychromatic silver, with chromium-plated mudguard and cowls, a dualseat, parking and stop lights, steering column lock, double shield protectors, horn cover, pillion footrests and a spare wheel as standard equipment, it sold for a modest £162 3s 10d.*

Above left *Veteran Douglas motorcycle rider Douglas Withers competed in the 1951 Pioneer Run to Brighton on the 696 cc 1907 V4 made by the Company at Bristol. He is seen getting a little help from two Vespa riders along the route. Mr Withers was the father of well-known Douglas personality, Eddy Withers, at one time Service and Competition Manager at the Kingswood works. Douglas Withers was very closely connected with the Norwood Motor Cycle Club and his enthusiasm for the Club is evident from the Club badge which can be seen on the front of his beret.*

Below left *Statistics show just how sales of Vespa peaked at the end of the 1950s and how in the early 1960s the 125 cc 152L2 and 150 Sportique models played their part in maintaining the popularity of scooters amongst the two-wheeler fraternity.*

The 150 cc Sportique model introduced in June 1961 proved one of the most popular machines ever made since Douglas first pioneered the post-war scooter movement in the UK. It was a four-speed machine with a revolutionary two per cent petroil mixture engine, which helped increase the performance and decrease engine carbon deposits. Available in a range of colours at £144 19s 9d it was described in a Scooter Weekly *article of 20 July 1961 as 'pretty good for such a well-equipped machine' and 'a good scooter made even better'.*

Below *The Grand Luxe version in a polychromatic colour known as Bahama Gold, fitted with a number of accessories, also became available. Both models carried the Douglas 12-month guarantee.*

Above *A new 125 cc model was introduced at the 1962 Earls Court Show, known as the 232L2. Generally as the Sportique, it had a smaller capacity engine and a three-speed gearbox. Very few were sold by the company and importation soon ceased.*

Vespa G.S.
SERIES II

TECHNICAL DATA

Max. Length . . . 70½″   Overall Height . . . 41½″
Dry Weight (including spare wheel) . . . 242 lbs.
Max. Width at handlebars . . . 28″

Cubic capacity: 158·53 c.c.   Bore: 58 m.m.
Stroke: 60 m.m.   Compression ratio: 7·3
Power: 8·0 b.h.p. at 6,500 r.p.m.

Engine: Two-stroke single cylinder—fan cooled—battery ignition.

Transmission: Direct.

Gear-Box: Number of Gears — 4.
Ratio — 1 : 14·72 — 1st   2 : 10·28 — 2nd
3 : 7·61 — 3rd   4 : 5·84 — 4th

Wheels: Interchangeable: 3·50 × 10.

Suspension: Front and rear helical spring with double acting hydraulic damper.

Brakes: Expansion type with flexible control cables.

Electrical: Fly-wheel magneto and battery feeding by A.C. — headlamp, main and dip beams, tail light. D.C. — parking lights, horn and stoplight.

STAR FEATURE . . .
. . . as standard equipment, this exclusive Luggage Compartment

DOUGLAS (SALES & SERVICE) LTD.
Kingswood, Bristol. Tel.: Bristol 67-1881.
A DIVISION OF THE WESTINGHOUSE BRAKE & SIGNAL CO., LTD.

Left *To satisfy the needs of the sporting fraternity with a desire to own a practical scooter with plenty of go, the 160GS was introduced in May 1962. The 150 model had earned a great reputation and with even more power and better acceleration, better suspension and a dualseat giving greater comfort, the 160GS proved a worthy successor to the 'Gran Sport' in its original 150 form. A spare wheel (now standard equipment) was fitted inside the cowl. A series II version of this popular scooter was introduced 12 months later with the luggage compartment moved to the inside of the front apron as shown in the leaflet giving details of this model.*

A lightweight model in the shape of the 90 Standard appeared in the spring of 1964, filling a gap in the range. Although the model maintained the traditional Vespa design features, considerable restyling had been applied both to the chassis and engine, with pleasing effect.

This cutaway section of the 90 power unit shows the advance design features and the amazingly compact layout of the engine. For technically minded readers, the 88.5 cc rotary valve engine delivered 4.1 bhp at 4,500 rpm.

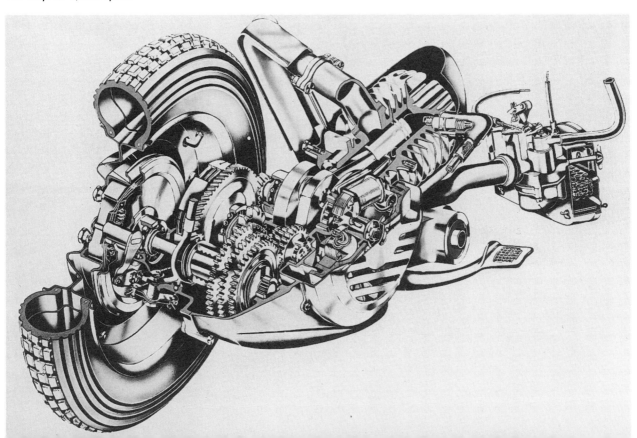

Left *At one of the very few provincial Motor Cycle Shows held outside of London, that held in Brighton 1965, the 90 Super Sport made its debut. It was introduced to satisfy the needs of those riders who preferred a sportier looking version of the 90. Motorcycle champion Derek Minter was pleased to give the new model an airing whilst visiting the Brighton Show.*

Below *This side view of the 90 SS gives an indication of the sporty appearance as compared to that of the Standard model introduced 12 months earlier. The centrally positioned spare wheel and the luggage and tool compartment plus a new exhaust system certainly made this a very attractive looking machine. It was finished in roma red, peacock blue or white.*

Above In his road impression of new models, Peter Fraser wrote in 24 February issue of Motor Cycle, 'If your need is for a willing little work horse for commuting or a poppy little playmate to share your leisure, the Vespa Super Sport 90 stands very high in the list of prospective partners.' Here Mike Kemp of the Hitchin Vespa Club is seen making a trouble-free ascent to the top of Agg's Hill in the under-150 cc class at the 1967 VCB National Rally sporting trial at Cheltenham. He seems to have found his 'poppy little playmate'.

Right A 90 SS being put through its paces by scooter sports rider Peter Hasler in the 1968 Isle of Man Scooter rally.

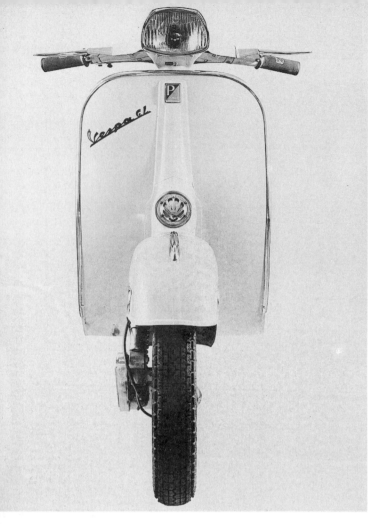

Left *A 150 model fitted with a new sleek, streamlined chassis and a squared-off headlamp was introduced at the May 1965 Blackpool Show. Fitted with a new rotary valve power unit it was known as the 150GL.*

Below *Here is a publicity shot of the 150GL. The model was withdrawn from the Vespa range with the introduction of the Sprint and SS 180 models.*

Right *A brace of SS models showing on the left the effect of two toning whilst the machine on the right is equipped with a range of accessories and fitted with a 12 volt electrical system for those who required more concentrated and powerful lights. It also enabled spot/fog lamps to be more efficiently operated and other electrical accessories to be fitted, if required.*

Below *Amongst the machines that proved so popular with Club members and sports enthusiasts was the 180SS model, from the day it was first imported in May 1965. Similar to the 160 model but with a bigger bore engine, higher compression ratio, streamlined styling and squared-off headlamp, the 180SS was one of the most exciting sports scooters to come from Vespa. This photograph was extensively used on much of the publicity material associated with the machine. A similar scene with Vespa Club Secretary Ian Kirkpatrick in the saddle, was used in VCB publicity.*

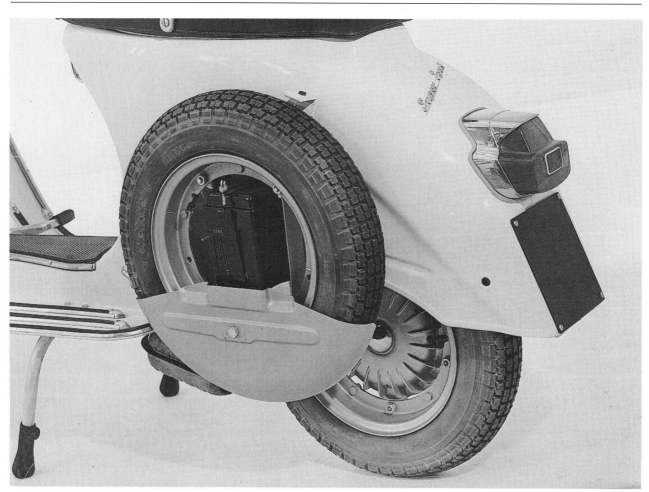

Above left *The Super Sport spare wheel mounting.*

Left *Front shield SS badge and headlamp.*

Above *The first of a new series was imported by the company in September 1965, known as the 150 Sprint. With a four-speed gearbox and 10 in wheels it was similar to the GL but had a higher compression engine and different gearing.*

Right *'Docile and willing' is what the press said of the Sprint. 'Responsive and easy to handle, it is a brilliant high speed touring machine of outstanding performance and acceleration.'*

Vespa AUTOMATIC FUELMIX

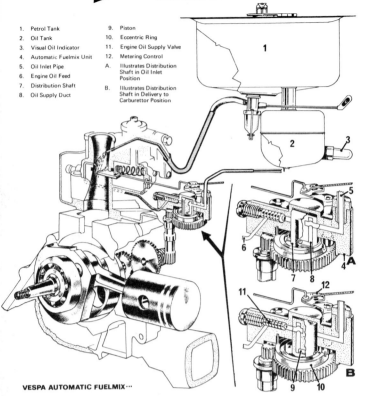

1. Petrol Tank
2. Oil Tank
3. Visual Oil Indicator
4. Automatic Fuelmix Unit
5. Oil Inlet Pipe
6. Engine Oil Feed
7. Distribution Shaft
8. Oil Supply Duct
9. Piston
10. Eccentric Ring
11. Engine Oil Supply Valve
12. Metering Control
A. Illustrates Distribution Shaft in Oil Inlet Position
B. Illustrates Distribution Shaft in Delivery to Carburettor Position

VESPA AUTOMATIC FUELMIX···

gives a constant predetermined petrol/oil ratio at all times. The unit is controlled by the throttle opening and is driven by the crank-shaft through a reduction gear and worm and pinion drive ensuring that the amount of oil delivered is consistent with the engine revs.

As the throttle is opened this brings into operation a variable eccentric which controls the amount of oil fed to the engine. The actual mixing of the petrol and oil takes place in the carburettor venturi before entering the crankcase.

THIS VESPA AUTOMATIC FUELMIX IS AVAILABLE AS AN OPTIONAL EXTRA ON THE VESPA 150 SUPER AND VESPA 150 SPRINT MODELS ONLY.

Douglas (Sales & Service) Ltd., Kingswood, Bristol. Telephone Bristol 671881

Division of the Westinghouse Brake & Signal Company Limited

17/5/68

Left The world's first scooter Automatic Fuelmix was available on the 150 Sprint and 150 Super models. It was the outcome of much research and trial testing by Piaggio to give a predetermined petrol/oil ratio at all times, the unit controlled by the throttle opening. For the technically minded, details are shown in the drawing.

Below The automatic Fuelmix was not available for fitting to existing machines as the two tanks necessary required a different chassis.

Right *The 150 Super of the VBC1 series was imported in the spring of 1966. It was similar in specification to the GL model but was fitted with 8 in wheels and had a different headlamp.*

Below *Whilst the demand in the mid-1960s was not as great for 125 cc models as for other capacity machines, the company introduced a 125 Series VMA1 in March of 1966. It was a temporary measure as a prelude to the importation of the 125 Primavera model in 1967.*

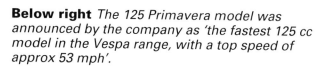

Below right *The 125 Primavera model was announced by the company as 'the fastest 125 cc model in the Vespa range, with a top speed of approx 53 mph'.*

Left During 1968 a number of 125 Super models were imported from the Spanish franchise holder, Moto Vespa, and here is seen one of the later models showing the front luggage compartment and mounting of the spare wheel.

Below left The successor to the 180SS was introduced into the range in 1970. Known as the 180 Rally it was designed for longer journeys and had a more powerful engine, for the sporting scooterist who required a higher performance machine. Its performance lived up to the name chosen. Unfortunately the same cannot be said of the 90 Racer. Whilst the company had high hopes of this model, sales were disappointingly low despite the fact that it was retained in the range for almost three years.

Above right A stablemate to the 180 Rally, the 200 Rally Electronic made its debut in November 1972. It was the top model in the Vespa range at £259. The Rally Electronic had a similar chassis to that of the 180 Rally but the claimed engine output was 12.3 bhp at 5,700 rpm.

Right Shortly after the introduction of the 200 Rally Electronic there followed the 50 VSA Series with 9 in wheels and a three-speed gearbox. It was fitted with pedals to comply with the moped regulations that existed at the time. In October 1973 it was followed by a model that lacked pedals, as shown. The Vespa 50 Special, introduced in 1977, superseded the 50N moped that was fitted with pedals.

Ciao

Spell it CIAO
Say it CHOW
Ride it NOW

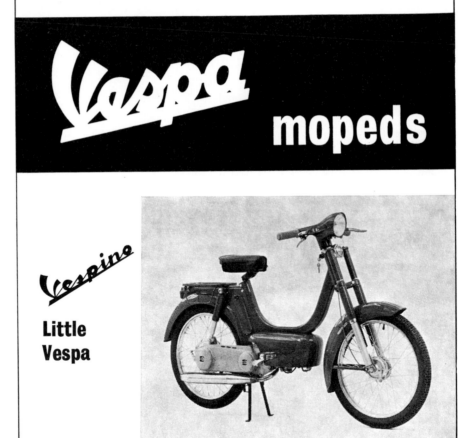

Vespino

Little Vespa

Whilst most readers will associate Vespa with scooters, having now referred to the Vespa 50 it is an appropriate time to make a reference to one or two other vehicles which have appeared in the Douglas price lists over the years. These machines were manufactured by Piaggio in Italy or by Moto Vespa in Madrid, Spain, and were handled by dealers as part of the Vespa franchise.

The Ciao moped from Italy and the Vespino models from Spain were well received when introduced in 1968. Over the years that followed many modifications were made to the single-speed engines and rigid frames of the earlier models. Here is a sample of the front cover of a Vespa moped sales folder.

Above *Three 'New Line' scooters were launched by Piaggio at an International Press ceremony at their Pontedera works in April 1978. Features of the new range included patented car-type suspension and damper units, flush fitting indicators and a 'New Line' style chassis. There was also a neatly designed luggage compartment, new handlebar layout, cowling, dualseat and a rear lamp, as can be seen from this angle shot.*

Right *A colourful 'New Line' catalogue was published by the company, on the front cover of which appeared these three riders and machines.*

Left *A model known as the Boxer was included in the range from 1971 to 1973 and six years later, in the spring of 1979, journalists from many countries were invited by Piaggio to Monte Carlo to witness a spectacular launch of a new model — the 'Si'. Those present saw the new model, suspended from a helicopter, drop to the landing pad at the Heliport, prior to the press launch in Monte Carlo's Sporting Club.*

Above right *Other 50 cc models were later included in the Vespa range. The PK50S models, with or without electric start, became available in 1983. The new sporty shape, indicators and useful luggage compartment are clearly visible in this photograph. The Roma 50 cc automatic model appeared on the Vespa (UK) stand at the 1986 Show. It had been designed so that both brakes were operated by handlebar levers.*

Below right *The 1980s saw further improvements and more new models. The PK and PX range was introduced in 1983. This is the PK125S model which had a kick starter. The new 125 PX125E also had a manually operated starter but incorporated oil injection via a separate, two-stroke oil tank. The biggest capacity Vespa in the range, the PX200E like the 125 PX125E had an oil injection system and a dualseat. It is interesting to note that a PK80S model embodying most of the features of the other models, but having an electric starter, was also included in the range.*

Left *Announced as the 1986 scooter sensation, the T5 model certainly made an immediate impression on Vespa riders. This 125 model with its dualseat, aerodynamic spoilers, wheel covers and 'tell-tale' instrumentation that included a digital rev counter certainly looked good.*

Below left *The new SFERA 50 automatic scooter launched by Piaggio (UK) in 1991, has greatly assisted lightweight sales in Britain. The Vespa 50 scooter reached the three million mark in 1991 and Piaggio with a production of nearly 800,000 scooters, mopeds, motor-cycles and three-wheelers were recognized as Europe's biggest two-wheel specialist.*

Above right *Unquestionably the star of the Vespa (UK) stand at the 1988 Motor Cycle Show was the sophisticated new Vespa Cosa model. It was announced that this model was currently undergoing homologation tests for the British market in preparation for its UK launch. This £16 million development benefited from many of the technological improvements which had been made in the two-wheel sector and added an element of Italian flair and panache to the original, world famous design.*

Right *No Vespa history would be complete without the inclusion of a number of photographs for which, chronologically, it would be difficult to find the correct place.*
Two great stalwarts of the Douglas service organization whose names were synonymous with Vespa amongst dealers and those Vespa Club members who attended rallies, were Ern Hendy and George Baber. Smiling Ern, seen here in a photograph which made the front cover of the October 1964 issue of Vespa News, *remains the sole survivor of the Douglas staff still active with Vespa.*

Left *George Baber, the other member of the Vespa service duo, is seen giving a Clubman model the once-over at an Isle of Man scooter rally.*

Below left *Georges Monneret, the patriarch of French motorcycle sport, will be long remembered for the many world records he held. Five days after his 43rd birthday in 1956, Monneret successfully crossed the English Channel from Calais to Dover in under six hours, on a Vespa specially mounted on floats. It was his second attempt as halfway across on his first, he struck a piece of driftwood and had to return to France with a badly damaged paddle.*

Above right *Oil giant Texaco introduced Tourist Pilots for a nine-week holiday period in 1970. Twelve girls dressed in sky-blue uniforms, riding 150 Super models, acted as guides in the Stratford-upon-Avon area. The Texaco Tourist Pilot scheme had started in Norway where it operated in five cities and had also run successfully in Sweden, to provide a free service to those who required any information or assistance in finding their way around a wide area of the surrounding countryside. Here is one of the Stratford-upon-Avon pilots ready to help.*

Right *With the co-operation of the Royal Automobile Club, a dual-control 125 machine was given an airing as seen here. The duplicate set of handlebar controls were operated by the instructor whilst the learner was left to do the steering.*

Left *During the 1960 Earls Court Show, the then Minister of Transport, Mr Ernest Marples, tried out a special Police machine fitted with a two-way radio. A number of police forces used Vespas, mainly for traffic control.*

Below left *Cmdr. W.J.A. Hollis inspecting the Nottingham Police Force.*

Right *The 150 Sprint Police model.*

Below *Shortly after the first Vespa rolled off the Kingswood production line a number of owners appeared to share a common interest by virtue of their attitude and way of looking at life. Possibly this is why, in the early days, scooter riders used to salute and wave to each other on the road. One of those riders who had the foresight to see the advantages of Vespa owners banding together and forming a club was a gentleman living in Watford, William Mitchell Bond. The Vespa Club of Great Britain will always be associated with Bill Bond, who founded the Club in 1952 with a few of his Vespa owner friends, to form the No 1 Branch. Bill Bond is seen here presenting to Lord Brabazon a Vespa Club badge and cuff links at the 1955 Motor Cycle Show.*

The ideal form of transportation, for sheer low cost economy, reliability, and easy maintenance the Vespa Police Scooter will aid the efficient running of any local authority.
For full details and demonstration, please write or telephone:
Special Services Department,
Douglas (Sales & Service) Ltd., Kingswood, Bristol.
Tel: Bristol 671881.
A division of the Westinghouse Brake & Signal Co. Ltd.

SPECIFICATION

FUEL CONSUMPTON APPROX 129 mls per gal of Petrol Oil mixture of 2% volume
MAX FUEL CAPACITY 1.7 imp gals including 0.3 imp gals reserve
RANGE APPROX 230 miles.   MAX SPEED APPROX 58 mls per hour

SIZES AND WEIGHT
WHEEL BASE   47.2 inches   HANDLEBAR WIDTH 26.3 inches
TOTAL LENGTH   69.6 inches   MAX HEIGHT   41 inches
MIN GROUND CLEARANCE 8.7 inches   TURNING RADIUS   55 inches
DRY WEIGHT with RADIO EQUIPMENT APPROX 200 lbs.

GEAR RATIOS
FIRST GEAR   14.46 to 1   THIRD GEAR   7.31 to 1
SECOND GEAR   10.28 to 1   FOURTH GEAR   5.36 to 1

ELECTRICAL EQUIPMENT
MILLER AC GENERATOR 22 AMP HOUR BATTERY HIGH OUTPUT RECTIFIER
HEAD LAMP 6 volt 25/25 watt bulb. STOP and TAIL LAMP with 6 volt 5 watt bulb
for Rear Light and Parking, 6 volt 10 watt bulb for Stop Lamp.
SPEEDOMETER LIGHT 6 volt 0.6 watt. PILOT LIGHT 6 volt 5 watt bulb.

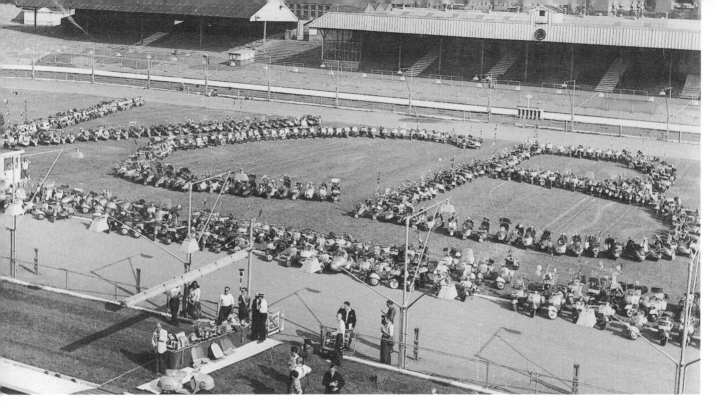

The aims and objectives of the Club were to promote the pastime and sport of Vespa scootering and to encourage social activities amongst those who had an interest in Vespa riding. It was not long before the advantages of becoming a member became apparent to the scooterist who had chosen a Vespa to ride. Through the enthusiasm of Bill Bond and his team it was not long before branches and regions of the Club were formed throughout the country. Club programmes were numerous and varied, and many friends were made through rallies which were well attended. The London Region held a most successful event at the Harringay stadium on Whit Monday 1960, this photograph showing quite clearly that the Concursio Vesparum Londinii was VCB hosted.

Whilst the Club today does not enjoy the much larger membership of the past, it continues to uphold the aims and objectives for which it has stood over the past 41 years. Having been associated with the VCB since its inception it gives the author great pleasure to record a few of the Club activities captured by the camera. The amount of space available allows only a very small selection of pictures to be included, which have been kindly loaned by members of the Club.
   The Annual Conference of the Club has been held at Leamington Spa since 1958, usually followed by a dinner and dance. This practice continues today. Here are members attending the 1959 Annual Conference where President Bill Bond welcomed the new General Secretary, Gerald Newton. A bi-monthly Club magazine — Vespa News — is produced and made available to Members. The Club is affiliated to the Federation Internationale des Vespa Clubs and the Federation of British Scooter Clubs.

'Pop' Muncaster was born in Poplar on 8 December 1884. A member of the South Essex Branch, he celebrated his Golden Wedding anniversary in July 1958. Pop joined the Club in 1953 and at 74 still rode his Clubman Vespa. He had retired in 1944 after completing 44 years service at Somerset House. Pictured outside the London Vespa Centre in Finchley Road is Pop with, from left to right, Charles Caswell of the Essex Club, Bill Bond and Claude McCormack.

Against a background of Club badges, newly appointed General Secretary Ian Kirkpatrick (**right**) is seen chatting to the Vice-President of the Club at the 1965 meeting. Ian joined the Glasgow Club in 1958, was a Scottish Region Council member in 1961/2 and the Competition Secretary.

Above left *One of the objectives of the Club is to promote sport and to encourage social activities amongst all who are interested in Vespa riding. This gathering of members of the Isle of Wight Club and their guests from the Thames Valley Club clearly proves the point.*

Left *Just how well attired a Vespa team looked.*

Above *Grass track events were popular at rallies and this photograph was often used by the company to promote the Vespa Club.*

Right *One of the early Bristol rallies was held in June 1956 and here are seen members assembled on Durdham Downs for a short service and blessing. Afterwards, they paraded through Bristol to a rally on the Sports Ground of the company at Kingswood.*

Since the first Isle of Man Scooter Rally in 1957 there has always been keen competition between Vespa and Lambretta scooter riders. In the early 1960s two of the sidecar champions were 'Bill' André, seen seated on the Vespa with French ace, André Baldet in the sidecar, who were also champions in 1960 and 1962. At the 1965 Rally, Vespa Club of Britain members claimed over 70 awards from an entry of 400 machines. Mike Murphy was 'Scooter King' and Elizabeth Smolen of Bebbington was crowned 'Scooter Queen'. In the 1969 Rally it was the 125 Primavera and 180SS models which featured prominently amongst the awards, whilst in the 1973 event the names of Norrie Kerr, Bob Young and Liz Chapple featured amongst the prize winners.

Douglas promenade on the Isle of Man makes an impressive background for the parade of Vespa Club riders competing in the 1958 Rally.

Above The driver in this rare photograph of a Vespa Rickshaw at the 1958 Isle of Man scooter rally is John Harris of the company sales team. He is seen here leading the parade of competitors along the promenade.

Right One of the star attractions of rallies was the riding ability of the Thames Valley Display Team, seen here performing in 1957. The team comprised from 10 to 15 Club members, including up to four girls, using two 42L2 Vespas suitably reinforced. Dressed in simple and effective display uniforms, with white safety helmets, they gave some very professional displays of trick and formation riding.

Members of the Thames Valley Display Team gave a very polished performance in front of the famous grandstand on the TT Course at the 1958 Rally. Some Team members are seen talking to 38-year-old German restaurateur L. Schwoerer, whose 1950 125 Vespa had 100,000 miles to its credit and was said to be the oldest machine in Germany.

A team of three 150 GS riders, André Baldet (58), Ken Harris (63) and Dennis Christian (69) were the winners of the 1959 IOM Manufacturers Team Award and are seen here with a few of their followers at the TT scoreboard.

William Bond, founder and president of the Vespa Club of Britain, celebrated his 70th birthday on Good Friday 1960. Bill is seen here proudly displaying his cards to his staff, Margaret Farquhar, Doreen Behan, and Secretary of the Club, Gerald Newton.

In London's 1960 Easter Parade at Battersea Park, half a million people went along to see the Grand Parade, amongst which were these specially decorated machines ridden by Club members.

Left *A popular event in which members of the Spalding Club participated was the Spalding Tulip Festival. Here Mary Brothwell is seen sitting amongst 12,000 tulip-heads, the Spalding Club's entry in the 1961 Festival. The insects with wings represent wasps — the Italian word for Vespa.*

Above *Four stalwart Vespa followers, from left to right: Donald Harris, London Area Sales Manager for Douglas, Charles Caswell and Dick Cumby, joint Council Members for the London Region and Gerald Newton, the VCB General Secretary.*

Below *Two competitors in the Team Event at the 1963 New Brighton, Cheshire Rally. Tony Thorpe of the Nottingham Club has been the backbone of this Club for many years. He is the Midland and Central Region Council Member, Vice-Chairman of the National Council, one of the VCB representatives of the Federation of British Scooter Clubs and a past Chairman of the Veteran Vespa Club.*

At the 1956 National Romford Rally, Don Merrett of the Thames Valley Club chats to a rather young-looking Charles Caswell. Could they have been discussing the possibility of turning the impromptu demonstration of six on a Vespa into the polished display team we were to see later?

The see-saw obstacle seen here being tackled at the 1966 Northampton Rally was a popular one in gymkhana events.

Above left *Peter Chapman of the Coventry club proudly holds aloft the Gymkhana Championship Trophy he won at the 1968 Cheltenham Super National Rally.*

Above right *Federation of British Scooter Clubs National Council Chairman David Smith, an old Vespa Club official and enthusiast, rides the 90SS once owned by Vespa Champion, Pete Chapman.*

Below *Members of the VCB team in the 1969 EuroVespa Rally held in the Italian city of Viareggio.*

Left The Veteran Vespa Club, membership of which is open to all owners of vintage and veteran machines, continues to increase and flourish under the Chairmanship of Leslie Smith and long-serving Secretary Frank Brookes, one of the founder members. Membership secretary and newsletter editor, David Hawkins of the Cheltenham club, and treasurer, Margaret Farquhar, have roots that go back to the very early days of the Club.

The first Veteran Rally was held in 1964. It was open to all Vespa scooters registered on or before 31 December 1954. The run started from Tattenham Corner at Epsom and ended in Brighton, and 37 machines took part. Here is Eddy Withers and his 1951 Italian-made 'Rod' model enjoying the Surrey air.

Below At the 8th Annual Rally of the Veteran Vespa Club a total of 40 machines participated. Here you see a line up of a few of them.

Leslie Smith of the Nottingham branch and Chairman of the Veteran Club, tackles the water splash in one of the six gymkhana events won by him on his 180SS at the 1967 Cardiff National Rally.

Well-known Thames Valley Club members Dot Hasler and husband Peter, photographed at the 1969 Isle of Man Scooter Rally. Dot won the Ladies Award with her fine riding in the Manx 400 and Night Semi-Sporting Trial, to become Scooter Queen.

BUCKINGHAM PALACE

13th July, 1977.

Dear Mr. Brockway,

I am commanded to convey to you and the Members of the Vespa Club of Britain the sincere thanks of The Queen for your kind message of loyal greetings on her Silver Jubilee which Her Majesty much appreciates.

Her Majesty congratulates your Club on its twenty-fifth anniversary.

Yours sincerely,

E. Brockway, Esq.

Left *A letter received from Buckingham Palace on the occasion of the Silver Jubilee of Her Majesty the Queen, which was also the 25th anniversary of the Vespa Club.*

Below *Over the years the Vespa Club of Britain has provided valuable assistance to the company in many ways and was always willing to help out on the Douglas stand at shows. Here at the 1977 Motor Cycle Show are seen Ern Hendy and Charles Caswell discussing a point of view, closely watched by the author and Ted Parrott, the* Vespa News *Editor. Charles Caswell took over the duties as the VCB General Secretary in 1970 until he relinquished the post at the 1991 Annual General Meeting when Clive Mills of the Maidstone Club assumed the responsibility for that duty.*

Right *Philips Electrical Ltd, sponsored for many years the VCB Championships and in the 1976 Vespa/Philips Super League the winners' trophy was presented to Norrie Kerr by the sponsor. Norrie, who was one of the leading scooter dealers in the country, is himself now the sponsor of the VCB/Mallosi UK/S&S Championship.*

Below right *The modern Vespa space men.*

CONCLUSION

The Vespa scooter has come a long way since those early Piaggio days and the involvement of Douglas, and in more recent years the involvement of Vespa (UK) Limited. In 1992 Piaggio Limited took over the franchise under the direction of Giuseppe Tranchina at their Orpington, Kent Headquarters. Production figures have been truly remarkable over the years. Sales world-wide in the first ten years had topped the 1 million mark and by 1961 they had doubled. By that time the Vespa was also being manufactured or assembled in Germany, France, Spain and Belgium, as well as by Douglas at their Kingswood works.

In 1969 the 4 million production mark had been reached and it is said that between 1948 and 1984 more than 7.25 million Vespas had rolled off the Pontedera production line. During the same period 1,150,000 had been manufactured under licence, with Douglas contributing a total of 126,230. Piaggio in 1991 had a sales turnover of £650 million when nearly 800,000 scooters, mopeds, motorcycles and three-wheelers were produced.

As the result of the Westinghouse acquisition of Douglas in 1957, the importation of machines from Italy and Spain continued, although the Vespa business was transferred to new premises on the Fishponds Trading Estate under the direction of the author and his sales and service team. It continued there until June 1982 when the transfer of the Piaggio franchise was made to Vespa (UK) Limited, a subsidiary of Two Four Accessories Limited, itself an autonomous subsidiary of Heron Trading Limited. It was located at Heron's purpose-built headquarters at Crawley in West Sussex. In August 1992 the formation of a British subsidiary — Piaggio Limited was announced after it was known the Crawley based Vespa (UK) Limited had given up the distribution of the Italian made scooter.

Today, some 47 years since Piaggio first introduced the Vespa scooter and over 44 years since its debut in the UK, the basic design has been modified only in detail, although there have been radical changes in engine design. It is therefore appropriate to pay a tribute to Ing Corradino D'Ascanio, its inventor, a truly remarkable man, and to Piaggio for making it all possible.

I doubt whether either D'Ascanio or Enrico Piaggio would have disapproved of the change in the design that came about with the introduction of the new range of Cosa, Sfera, Zip, Quartz and Free mopeds and scooters. Who would dare predict Vespa's future in the 1990s?